MUSIC MAKERS

Trumpets

by Cynthia Amoroso and Robert B. Noyed

Watch three fingers move quickly up and down. See the light shining off the horn. Hear the sound. Toot, toot, toot. He is playing the trumpet.

A trumpet player moves his fingers while playing.

A trumpet is a **wind instrument** made of metal **tubing**. The metal is curved in an oval shape.

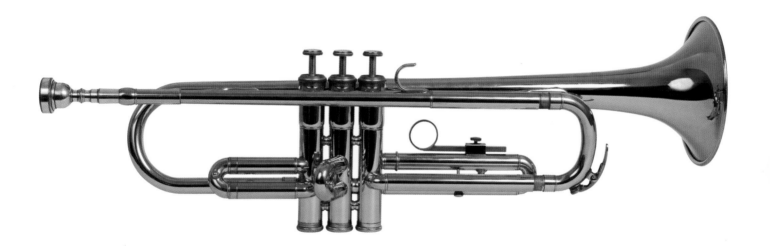

A trumpet is long with rounded ends.

A trumpet is played with the mouth. A player blows air through the trumpet. Then sound comes out the other end of the trumpet.

A boy plays a holiday song on his trumpet.

The end of the trumpet has a big opening. The metal flares out. This part is called the **bell** because it has a bell shape.

A trumpet player plays in a mariachi band.

There are three keys on the trumpet. These keys are called **valves**. A player makes different sounds by pushing the valves.

The middle three fingers press the valves.

A player makes sounds by changing the shape of her mouth, too. The lips **vibrate** while playing the trumpet.

A girl moves her mouth to play the right note.

The trumpet is an old instrument. People in China played a kind of trumpet thousands of years ago. Now trumpets are played all over the world.

This trumpeter plays in Latin America.

Trumpets are important to many people. Long ago, people used them to make announcements. Today, trumpets are usually played to make music.

This trumpet is part of a street band.

Trumpets are important for many kinds of music. Many trumpet players are famous for **jazz** music. Children play trumpets in school bands.

School marching bands have trumpets.

Toot, toot, toot. Playing the trumpet is so much fun!

A girl practices the trumpet.

Glossary

bell (BEL): A bell is the end of a trumpet that is shaped like a bell. A trumpet's sound comes out of the bell.

jazz (JAZ): Jazz is a type of music that is lively and rhythmic. Jazz music can be played on a trumpet.

tubing (TOOB-ing): Tubing is long, hollow pipe. Trumpets are made of metal tubing.

valves (VALVZ): Valves are movable parts that are pressed on a trumpet. A trumpet has three valves.

vibrate (VY-brayt): Things that move back and forth very quickly vibrate. A trumpet player's lips vibrate.

wind instrument (WIND IN-struh-munt): A wind instrument is an instrument that uses air to make sound. A trumpet is a wind instrument.

To Find Out More

Books

Curnow, James. *Classics for the Young Trumpet Player.* Wilmore, KY: Curnow Music Press, 2003.

Pipe, Jim. *How Does a Trumpet Work?* Brookfield, CT: Copper Beech Books, 2002.

Web Sites

Visit our Web site for links about trumpets: *childsworld.com /links*

Note to Parents, Teachers, and Librarians: We routinely verify our Web links to make sure they are safe and active sites. So encourage your readers to check them out!

Index

About the Authors

Cynthia Amoroso has worked as an elementary school teacher and a high school English teacher. Writing children's books is another way for her to share her passion for the written word.

Robert B. Noyed has worked as a newspaper reporter and in the communications department for a Minnesota school district. He enjoys the challenge and accomplishment of writing children's books.

On the cover: A trumpet band plays on a sidewalk.

Published by The Child's World®
1980 Lookout Drive • Mankato, MN 56003-1705
800-599-READ • www.childsworld.com

ACKNOWLEDGMENTS
The Child's World®: Mary Berendes, Publishing Director
The Design Lab: Design and production
Red Line Editorial: Editorial direction

PHOTO CREDITS: Joe Brandt/iStockphoto, cover; iStockphoto, cover, 3, 5, 15; Terry Healy/iStockphoto, 7; John Stelzer/iStockphoto, 9; Rick Lord/iStockphoto, 11; Anita, Patterson/iStockphoto, 13; Andrey Butenko/iStockphoto, 17; Gina Smith/Shutterstock, 19; Hannes Elchinger/Shutterstock, 21

Printed in the United States of America in Mankato, Minnesota.
November 2009
F11460

LIBRARY OF CONGRESS CATALOGING-IN-PUBLICATION DATA
Amoroso, Cynthia.
  Trumpets / by Cynthia Amoroso and Robert B. Noyed.
     p. cm. — (Music makers)
  Includes index.
  ISBN 978-1-60253-357-8 (library bound : alk. paper)
  1. Trumpet—Juvenile literature. I. Noyed, Robert B. II. Title. III. Series.
ML960.A46 2010
788.9'219—dc22   2009030209